Published by Polari Press
polari.com @polaripress

ISBN: 978-1-914237-17-1

Printed by TJ Books using vegetable
inks on 80gsm FSC paper. Typeset in
10/12 Roslindale.

Cover design and typesetting
by Peter Collins for Polari.

This first edition was printed in
the UK in March 2024.

WE ARE HUNGRY FOR ANDROGYNY

LEILAH KING

polari

Contents

I

WOMEN IN SUITS

Women in Suits

aqua jacket, shirt unbuttoned
matching trousers
train home chinos
acid green top, leather satchel
got on the tube, barely legal
scruffy jeans, band hoodie
bronze skin, fresh meat
inked-up kohl
hold contact, septum piercing
butch hero, your smile is arming me
we are hungry for androgyny
awkward teens, big town
baby gay, late Saturday
lost in a throng, up the country
waistcoat, mixed-race
Farsi-speaking, proof of freedom
tomboy T-shirt, boyfriend jeans?
crossdressing cruisers
skater girl, baggy jumper
shaved head, mystery body
stoned skin tone, unknown monotone
voices trying to find a home

Estranged

One day I woke up
to the smell of coffee in the percolator.
The sun pouring in through the window
the offering of love as it was.
I woke up and decided I can't survive here.
The clannishness is alluring.
The space they left for me
to be a woman, to be demure, to not swear, to find a husband.
If you can do that you can enjoy this space;
if you can do that you can come home,
you can sit safely in my arms.
My whole life was an ultimatum,
one I had to sever slowly with blunt aplomb.

Lezbo

QUEER. My love, call me your woman.
I lay my head in a quiet space
softly on petals, our bed is white and the door is closed.
BUTCH. When we met we were both wearing purple.
We're sat on the embankment under the summer hue.
I asked if I could kiss you.
DYKE. We went to Cornwall for your birthday,
you wanted to swim in the sea before breakfast,
it was January, we ran together in the rain.
I held your towel and waited in the shallow.
LEZBO. I was scared of meeting your family.
How could I be enough?
Bunched up in sleeves and braced for impact.
MASC. I get misgendered by strangers.
I don't mind, let's ignore them together.
MANLY. I have manly hands, that's what she said
in Brighton. That place reminds me of winter.
UGLY LESBIANS. I am beautiful when I'm with you.
IN LOVE. You make me feel in love. I love you.

Tracy Chapman

When I was younger I wrote in code,
every romantic note was nameless and alone.
I am talking about the days of gaydar,
the days of no gays for days,
where the light split through the shades like a headache.
I'm sat by the sad computer screen and the dresser
my dad spent the weekend painting.
I met this Canadian woman on the internet.
We spoke for a few years but I never set foot
in her orbit, her life in Vancouver.
I remember getting drunk at my friend's talking to her
in the middle of fuck-wheat nowhere
I felt so shit surrounded by lil goth boys with hard dicks.
That night we overheard someone getting a BJ,
to Tracy Chapman, so we sang along,
childlike jeers in the bathroom,
moving back and forth in the tub.
Someone get me an out, fast
car from here – a ticket to anywhere.

Bristol Butch Bar

It's political – being you.
You don't realise it;
to say so seems loud and gaudy.
But it's true and there's not one way,
soft, strong, stud, trans, femme, masc, nonbinary,
unidentifiably – society will probe
leaving scars.
But not here; each week the numbers grow,
bring your friends, bring crew cuts, mod-rock, denim,
    leather,
I don't give a fuck.
You will be appreciated and sometimes it's hard to admit
how unfamiliar that feels,
but we got you butches, we've been there too.

Blossom

It's time to put your washing outside.
The sky's finally dry
like your eyes after months of downpour.
Assemble the outfits with steady hands
that are whittled and grilled like hanging meat.
Starchy white body shapes inertly drape,
garments hold your body in place like bandages.
There's a blossom tree peeking,
peeking over the wall.
It shudders mouthfuls of petals.
I stand on them, wading through.
Will I bloom, will I find my form among them?
Discarding yesterday's fray,
I am a bruised and blood-soaked woman.

Man-Hating Lesbian

You hit on my girlfriend
in my front room on my birthday.
You talk over my poetry set
and argue with me about what I meant.
You attack me on the football pitch
after I 'humiliate' you.

You attack me
when I use the women's toilet;
you try to kick down the door, shouting obscenities.
You grab me by the collar and call me a dyke.

You denigrate my existence
and treat me as a threat,
you exhaust me constantly
and try to take away my dignity.

You call me a man-hating lesbian
to my friend at a party.
I am trying to like you
but you make it impossible.

The GNC

We had tickets to see a band; it was snowing.
The gig was on the corner of the queer quarter.
I ordered us four beers, so we wouldn't have to queue
    again.
I needed to pee, so ran out.
I dove into the toilet stall, trying not miss the last song.
As I walked back down the stairs
a man's hand grabbed my shoulder, with a shove.
I jolted, nearly losing my feet in the stairwell;
the rest was a blur. The guy, a valiant vigilante,
interrogated my gender, voice, clothes, my need to use the
    girls' loo.
He was alerted by his girlfriend,
who heard my masculine extractions,
looking to be rescued.
She was watching it unfold, scanning my body for clues.
We went at it, with the bouncer too,
so I asked for the manager and went up to his room.
We stepped into his office, I started explaining
and I couldn't stop crying, alone with this bloke,
four grimy walls and music thudding in the background.
He started moving and asked me to come with him.
We met the pair at the stairs and the manager pointed at a
    poster,
ZERO TOLERANCE OF DISCRIMINATION,
and he kicked them out, just like that.
She looked so shocked when her boyfriend had to fetch
    their coats.
I went to the bar, and watched them walk away in the
    snow.

Dyke Drill

dine out dyke
fetish fuck
subversive slut
stranger stone
kebab kink
lipstick lust
make me drink
disconnect
angry, lucid
crush contained
love for rent
rude girl's bent
churlish chaps
body out
trim my bush
doppelganger
you're not special
reel it in

It's Them

I knew from a young age that I was unpopular.
Disliked, invisible but visibly jarring.
Put in my place, taught to not value myself.
I wasn't sure what they despised exactly:
my nose, my manliness, my foreign family. I was just a kid.
I didn't know how this was meant to go.
Fast-forward to my twenties, working my first job,
being told how unattractive I am – professionally?
I am so used to being dismantled casually,
I didn't know how to stand up for myself.
Being told how unlikeable I am,
being told, being told.
I read a poem by Audre Lorde.
I watch a queer movie alone in the dark.
I fall in love, I learn our history
and try to unlearn them.
I read the words on the back of my diary:
It's not you, it's them.
It's not you, it's them.
It's them.
It's them.
It's them.

Pride

You stand proudly as a butch woman.
Repeat after me:
I am not a burden.
I will trust, I will find community.
My friends like me.
They hold my lungs afloat to keep me breathing;
their voices and stories echo a lifetime of silence.
Every time we internalise a world
that we cannot change, we see the space dwindle.
Hands age from fighting to survive.
Our pride is seen as unjustified.
You are just, you deserve love.
Repeat after me:
you are just, you deserve love, and safety.

II

MUM'S HOUSE

Mum's House

It was a time of teen nihilism.
Arms wrenched around a sink,
I stooped and puked on the carpet,
saw my breath on the taps and stared at the ceiling.
I could hear my mum making rice, slicing lamb.
It was hot; she had the skewers on
to be scorched in strips in the garden,
the *ssses* melting into birdsong.
And when he was home, my dad picked apples and made
    pudding
which lay uneaten in the freezer with the ready meals and
    the pizza.
We were more interested in night;
sneaking limbs opened creaking doors.
Snuck trousers tucked into socks, sockets turning
    blood-red;
it was more appealing than life,
and she slept heavy
under a darkness that was unruly.
She was always cold. I wanted to protect her,
so at night I tried to put my feet on hers
to keep them warm.

McDonald's, McDonald's, Kentucky Fried Chicken and a Pizza Hut

Mum took us there when we were little
on days off in between watching Disney,
little blots of rain and little coats.
The city seemed mammoth to her.
The girl from Shiraz
under the gold M, arterial gates.
She never said it
but you thought it seemed novel to her,
this Western thing,
cattle market excited,
stuck to your chair
with barbecue lips
and your mum's faded nail varnish,
olive skin sculpted hands,
hold me, mâmân.
She never said it
but it seemed novel and special to her,
little blots of rain
on days off in between watching Disney
when the city seemed mammoth.

Shiraz, City of Poets

Shiraz is a rich city, the capital of Fars,
my mum's birthplace,
a bustling space of cigarette smoke and bazaars.
I watch the women speak in the kitchen while they prepare
  khoresh
and if forgotten I repeat *mâmân, mâmân, mâmân*.
Shiraz is the city of poets;
while here you become romantic,
impulsive, light but full of food, skin enviably dark.

I want you to love me.
I want you to accept and cherish me as I am.

I am here with Hafez and Saadi Shirazi;
my body is among the blue mosaic,
among a thousand pieces of smashed glass
to rest in the reflection of Shāh Chérāgh.
Surrounded by fierce women.
The men are dancing, the night is warm, there is a fever,
a stranger kisses my face.
Alone in an unmade bed
my blood surrendered to distant memory.

Grandma

You'd say, *Hello*.
I'd say, *Salam*,
if I wasn't feeling shy.
My grandma was a matriarch, humorous and light.
She raised my mum, who was one of nine;
they lived in Shiraz in the house that we visited.
I don't remember meeting my granddad;
there are stories and pictures.
When I was young, she came to visit.
We took her to Blackpool to see the sea.
I remember her wearing a long black headscarf, walking
    through the street.
We strolled tightly together, arms interlocked;
the wind moved the fabric underneath her feet.
I remember her sleeping in the dining room
on the fold-out bed; I got into it with her, wrapped between
    her legs.
We didn't speak the same language, but I love you,
    Grandma,
dooset daram azizam.

Caspian Sea

We stand in a zigzag queue, wearing pale jeans and black
    headscarves;
the afternoon light is piercing white and the sky is
    patchwork blue.
I can't get the stone to skim the waves like you do.
The photos have faded, the Caspian Sea is a faint memory.
I stare, yearning to belong.
The women on the beach are gated by a single rope away
    from the men;
we stick to our section and I keep my clothes on.
We arrived the night before, driving through tunnels.
Passing Veresk Bridge, the mountains were a black lake
only interrupted by your reflection.
I fell asleep on my cousin's lap,
all piled in together into our uncle's space cruiser.
We arrive at the beach house to sleep for the night
but I stir, stepping over limbs.
The loungers are still out, the poker cards turned up,
there is a sliver of orange soda left in an ornate sapphire
    glass.
I sit down, hold my legs close to my chest
and watch the ocean wash away.

Running in Shiraz

My uncle Javad took me to a running track
with my cousin who couldn't keep up.
I love my uncle;
he would kiss my cheeks and sing to me.
He loved how green England was
and when he visited he would walk up the mountain every
    day
greeting the passers-by.
Now years later I get up early,
stretch my knee, gently roll my ankles rhythmically,
and I think about him and my cousins.
Playing football in the park in Shiraz with these boys we
    met,
driving on the motorway with the windows down
under lights and whirling arches.
My cousin instructing me to stand in the shade;
I would always refuse, burning red.
I woke up this morning alone, put my shoes on
and left the house to go running,
moving rapidly under the trees,
saying hello to the people I'd meet.

Diaspora Woman

I want to disappear.
To be stripped back like a forest full of hairs
plucked pure, to a simple skeleton.
Prime from the distress of being worn like an apron.
Your mother fancy, the bed is empty,
my blood is vandalised like a plot in an allotment,
the remnants of good intentions.
Ah, to be an empress, with feet that are delicate.
Ah, the perception, the violent punishment.
I cannot stomach you, your feasting is waspish,
my tongue is swollen and unable to roll her language.
We're not the women you ordered,
we're not the daughters you wanted.

My Mother

You are sat next to your sister driving through Shiraz.
Marvash's smile is identical to yours.
You put the phone out of the window to show me the passing
    cornfields;
yellow and green whirl past
under the magnetic heat of a lost summer.

You arrive back in England; you have four full suitcases.
Inside there's pistachio, sabzi, gaz and bracelets you ask me
    to try.
The jewellery feels too beautiful
so we settle on a sachet of saffron and a book of poetry.

You're in a grainy video, you must be in your twenties,
striking dark eyes and a bob haircut; you are laughing on a
    dusty patio.
I can't place the youthful man in the background
wearing cream linen with a full dark beard.

You are holding me,
I'm a baby, we are sat on seven Persian rugs
that are matched together like pieces of the Caspian Sea.
Sapphire green meets azure blue in darkened pockets
of heat you step through; there are pieces missing, exposing
    the cold stone floor.

Burden

Her life was made smaller by men,
outbursts punching down,
hands crumpled,
breasts held,
squashing, simpering,
boiling over in a cauldron of bademjhan.
I'm trying to find something to stand on
to help her stir the cumin
I escape – *ah*, *ah*, I have tried to escape the perception.
Through scalding, I have lost empathy,
running through water, jumping over fire,
into sabzi's bitterness.
I put my feet down alone to lay roots.

Intimacy

craving intimacy
fading in and out like water on sand
to be still, listening, are you listening to the ocean?
are you strong for the swell?
can you swim through your neglect?
love is nestled in photos
it's not like I can forget
trying to express words like old milk
I am not sure what I'd say
knocking the stuffing out of a cowboy
brutalising Barbie, stuck in stinging nettles
she's a fixer, fixing on sickness
I want to mend, mend
will you mend me?
sewing my mouth shut
pulling up into the driveway

Fish and Chips

fried smell
battered skin
single sachet
Friday night
ketchup, mayo
small forks are temporary toothpicks
can of Coke, tub of curry
weekends in Britain
rain on sea
second-hand car
music on cassette
putting chewing gum in my hair
old news fades into me

You Ask Me About Iran

January 2023

I reveal too much.
Feeling a sadness fall over me like winter.
It's a grainy picture,
a familiar roadblock,
oceans separating a sense of who I am.
Forced into a numbing distance, a pariah.
Certain of the pervading feeling of hopelessness.
I am sat at dinner sharing,
muted by conspiracy and history.
Privileged birthplace,
faux family, muddled heritage.
All I sense is the fear and futility of womanhood.

III

LETTER FROM MY THERAPIST

Letter from My Therapist

it may concern Leilah
for a year together
we explored her origin and family
childhood experiences that undoubtedly
led to PTSD
this negatively impacts her presently
her ability to cope with stress and anxiety
she has taken enormous steps
developing coping strategies
but life acts against further change
a lack of support and a tendency to be undermined
relating to her identity and her state of mind
means she can be triggered into
patterns of impulsive self-destruction
if she feels affected by discrimination
she can find it hard to use her head
and review her options
and the consequences of her actions
she is committed to working through things
given the time and space she needs

Awkward Dancing

is like laughing at a funeral
is like trying to fuck a letterbox
is like getting competitive with your own children
is like getting what you want after behaving appallingly
is like trying to pretend you are cultured by putting on an
    accent
is like going to an orgy to picket for chastity
is like making a room full of people listen to your poetry
awkward dancing is when you are too aware of your own
    body
where it follows you around like you have dirt in your eye
skittishly looking to copy others and their plumage shuffle
    which seems right
awkward dancing
is where people whisper things into your ear like
are you OK?
don't worry, no one's watching
but dancing is different when I am with you
clinging to your shoulders
at first reassuring me
I let go slowly to look at the ceiling, yes, I am still breathing
you hold my hand
I am allowed to be here

Realisation

Written during a hypomanic state, 2010, Brighton

I had a moment of realisation
that my simple words could not fashion
as I started to decay,
a meagre twenty-one years
conveying the frailty of losing my way.
But this realisation truly reflected
that when losing one's way the help of others should not
    be neglected,
respected, inflicted, reciprocated, hated,
weighted in hypocrisy, twisted into demise and lies,
no more tears to cry.
I dedicate my realisation
and the strengthening of my spine and the poisoning of
    your wine
to a depraved insidious encroachment of anger and
    insecurity that afflicts us all.
A blind man is not truly blind;
a high man is living a lie because he cannot see
that I have actualised, realised and surmised
that his eyes are truly blind.

Just Noise

Written during a depressive state, 2011, Bristol

I want to fight or fuck;
it's the same, I'm just noise.
It makes me feel wanted either way.
My body is empty,
hands empty, fists empty;
there's longing to feel it,
to feel fought, and ravaged by a sense of being,
of triumph, only empty.
Dry palms greet my pride,
full from boredom's need.
Base desires to digest on lonely walks home,
the moonlight on your back weighing your bones in
    quicksand.
Frostbitten skin leaves love bites where her lips should be;
your cold heart is trembling in a lonesome hood.
I want to fight or fuck;
it's the same, I'm just noise.
It makes me feel wanted either way.

Plenty of Fish

2011, Bristol

The internet, a pool of void people,
a pool to be destroyed by the insecure and deceitful.
There's plenty more nothing to behold, be held, hold me.
Hold on to your brighter side, an angle that's favourable
    between your thighs.
That's classy, right? I had to drink plenty classy glasses of
    wine to be here tonight.
I didn't realise I was staring down the barrel of a fool.
She talked about her spiritual side, her Rastafari
    appreciation of the moon
and how she had all the space to room another
with things we said to each other, as one thing led to
    another,
then we lay in bed and spooned together.
3am lucid liquid dreams I pretend,
I can't sleep, I stare at this stranger embraced in such
    remnants of intimacy
as nothing really remains inside me.
It's like desire lines are carved between our naked body
    lines
reflected by moonlight's wisdom. Flings can be fun, but
    what, when, who, why?
And beauty does indeed deceive the eye,
and as sure as a wavering mirage
I dismiss her distasting visage as I wring my eyes shut,
strangling reality's darkness.
6am light loomed brightly lit, white filled the room as
    frightful magnified silence ensued.
*You better leave, she said. Yeah, but my ticket isn't scheduled
    till two,*
but who are you and what was last night?

Naivety set in sex and love are not the same thing
and my synonymous expectation of meeting skin and
    minds and thoughts within
are not the same, and souls always feel heavier anyway
and not so lightly led; haste and shame did meet in bed
in networking through strangers' nets.
Embarking through this mindless medium I met myself,
this shallow, insecure, deceitful being.
By muddying with brighter wiles, I use lighter lies from my
    dark side to sleep at night.
To behold, be held, hold me tight.

Anxiety

Anxiety is a boring word,
is loaded, overused,
twangy, latent, permanent,
impermanent, inexplainable.
Some days I wake and feel it.
I try to shake it off and understand,
frozen limbs, the heightened wall,
the harshness of everything.
Your eyes are listless, your manner irritated,
your sweat is a tide, it falters your stride
or makes you puff out your chest.
You choose the wrong words, the words are always wrong,
you are never right. There is a constant fear of fight or
    flight.
She told me a story about a tiger.
The tiger escaped from Russia, but somehow it has
    boarded a ship
and somehow it's headed to you and somehow you left
    your door open
and in some way your mind will find a method to torture
and someday you will find peace
and someday the body will learn to be still.

A Full Night's Sleep

sleep hygiene
we read
consists of denying
yourself numbing agents
do not
watch TV in bed
drink too much booze
get scared or excited
that night we had a bath and did all the things we needed to
I woke up like the night before
under the summer dawn
weary and dirty
stumbled into another room
comfort escapes me

Not Feeling Lonely, but Being Alone

When we first met, I had to vet every thought;
every interpersonal chat required mediation.
I had no inner trust of who I was and what I needed
and how to speak freely.
After years of therapy, I am getting better
at accepting my quirks and the risk
that comes with making mistakes,
getting to know someone, not taking on their shit.
Conversely I have no issue with being unpopular
with people I despise, do not trust, or have no interest in.
We'd embark on normal group situations, usually with
    men,
where I would be flush with acerbic rhetoric with no care
    for them
and the quiet consequent discomfort I caused everyone.
But I am trying to be more kind and understand their
    threat.
I am a secret introvert and it clutters my mind.
My therapist told me much of the hurt
the world is awash with
stems from society's obsession with extroversion
and I do my bit, with a peacock beak persona,
but sometimes I don't know how else to be here,
and it is funny and it feels powerful.
But if I can get past this and feel grounded,
calm and recover from the harm I experience,
I will free myself to be truly strong,
not feeling lonely, but being alone.

Untitled

Sunday ritual, coffee, magazine, the cat.
I have made a plan to fill,
searching for acceptance,
making peace with shame,
hold, let it pass, say it out loud.
I am getting better at understanding the grasp of you
still feeling sorry while you stand on my throat.
We speak different languages
so I use your silence and then inevitably
I am sorry, I am sorry, I am sorry
I didn't turn out that way.

That's Not an Apology

I'm sorry you feel this way.
I'm sorry you interpreted it that way.
You got me wrong.
You have misunderstood me.
You're too sensitive.
I hear you, but

We ask for apologies, but why?
To hear five letters, bravely confronting the
    embarrassment
of getting something wrong.

I'm sorry, I care about you and I didn't mean to impact you in
    that way.
I know, that sounds really difficult.
I hadn't realised, but I understand now. Let's start over.
I want you to know how much I love you. I will make sure I do
    things differently.
I value you and what you have been through.
OK, I apologise, I had not thought of it like that. Can I give you
    a hug?

The Right Light

After years of ruminating,
cast under a spell of silence, my body is rocking back and
    forth,
developing traumatic stretch marks.
I am glistening like sand soaked by the ocean,
punctured by rubbish and other people's footsteps.
I do not have any more patience.
I do not have to make you feel comfortable while you make
    me squirm.
When I walk I imagine falling into a well,
when I cycle I imagine being dragged under a lorry.
When I speak to you my confidence crumbles.
A stranger asks me in the kitchen if I am OK.
Out of nowhere my mind has now ordered everything
    neatly.
I am tired because...
I am holding on to myself.
It sounds like I feel loss when I write this down,
but I am trying to win, and rebuild the things that are left.
Like ruins, I am beautiful in the right light.

IV

OVERHEARING

Overhearing

Overhearing your words.
They wash over me like saltwater,
poach skin like a pear.
I don't recognise how you see me.
I read somewhere that you are in control of your own
    destiny.
I am thinking this as I argue with a man in a phone shop.
Lost at sea, land slipping into fires,
islands cut apart by motorways and new street names.
I heard that if you have a bad relationship with your family
it can make it difficult to form connections.
I am trying,
having a conversation in the pub,
truly laughing.
I can see myself in the mirror, in the moment.
There's not one way to mend.

Dear Mr Referee

Performed as a song

In the world
there are rules.
There's a hierarchy of victim.
If you look like me, a little bit scruffy, a little angry,
when you play on the field
you don't get much slack from him.
You don't get much humanity.
If a pretty little girl with flicky blonde hair kicks me in the leg
the referee says, *Play on! Thank you, God.*
If I do anything marginally competitive, I am going to go to jail,
because I am fucking with the binary and he wants me to go
    to hell.

Rescue Dog

I woke up and took you
out into the blackened night.
We were alone with the faint flow
of your zigzag toes
tapping with chaotic abandon.
I don't know how to care for you;
another life's crept in all of a sudden.
She would have wanted you
to be safe and suited to the new humans.
Here we are, just like the morning sun,
as if I knew you were coming.

Morning

In the morning our egos settle
in slanted beds made from twisted metal.
The rotten moth-eaten cotton
turns pink skin brittle.
So you rise earlier than wanting
while petrichor listens;
she's still there
on the dry earth – she glistens,
softening the hum,
entering, pressing the pane.
I don't want be dressed, she murmurs.
I want to regress to naked nothingness
or something less violent than red nylon
or what it means to be a woman.
In the morning you feel the calm – still
like a tremor
forced by a stranger's hand – still,
not knowing who, not knowing.
The morning is subtle,
empty and beautiful.

Football

I scored to the rapturous roar of *well done, love*
and a group of them chastising their friend for being
  beaten by a girl.
His response was a causal scissor kick to my left knee.
I guess that's what you call equality;
you can't have it both ways, mate.

Valentine

I saw a bulge of blokes bunched
around the rose section at Tesco.
Carefully cruising hands over red buds,
long stems wrapped magnificently.
Attached were pre-written expressions of love.
I wondered if these were the men who belittled their wives.
Who were threatened by strong partners,
who watched Andrew Tate,
who told women to smile,
whose jealousy and entitlement turned violent like a light
    switch.
Who taught minorities they need
to be pliable and accommodating to stay safe.
Who would stand by when strangers objectified teenage girls,
adult men who want to fuck women who look like teenage girls.
I wondered how the world became
so bleak and backwards and old-fashioned.
I caught the eye of a guy scanning the flowers
and smiled automatically,
not wanting to offend a system that wants to harm me.

Friend

The sun sets on Rosie's allotment.
We're sat on opposite ends of the bench
with tinnies and cigarettes.
My hands are wound tightly;
the plot is wild green.
We become lost in strapped plants and blackberries
that lean unnaturally.
We are unruly – not fitting in beautifully.
I want to compliment your short hair,
I want to be still and truly hear you,
but today I am tired and frayed.
I wonder if you notice
the moon beating down on us.
I settle slowly
feeling calmed by my friend.

Smile

I got told by a big man
that it's a nice morning
so I should smile more.
So I braced my body and bit my tongue
and furrowed my brows and hunched my shoulders
and made myself more and more
like a slab of rock,
a dour colour, irreverent as fuck.
I had to fight the old me
who would hold his eye
and hold his view and make it mine
and somehow apologise for being human
and somehow apologise
for not being his kind of woman.

Stray Cats

We have stopped counting the cats on our holiday.
We blow them kisses instead
and let them sit suggestively close at dinner.
The men seem kind here,
leaving bowls of dried food and water for the felines.
It must be the sun on his face,
the absence of machismo,
the freedom of feeling
and the slower pace.

The Pandemic

I stand at the window and watch
the heavyset men gather suspiciously
around the park workout equipment.
It is taped up 'prohibited';
so are the swings.
No swinging for you, butty.
Your muscles are not the exception,
the exceptional men from the government tell them.

Bristol Roller Derby

roller skates, four wheels
inked up, black eyes
world map, left thigh
throwing shade, crashing light
skirting crunch, screeching twist
waxed floors, flailing fists
woman brakes, circular grace
delicate accelerant, brave face
blocker brute, patched up
fall out, keep pace
war paint, knee brace
match won
derby day

England Lose the Euros, 2020

Everyone's off sick,
the streets are littered with shit,
heroes have become enemies.
A man stands in the middle of the road with an England flag
willing the bus to hit him.
Everyone is an expert,
an armchair athlete.
The fans are fickle;
they cry and laugh and smash their wives.
It doesn't change anything,
just the walk home, the late bus ride
after the tough times.
You put all your eggs in last night.
Hold yourself tight, England;
hold your tongue, stay inside.

Rainbow Flags

Cold men eat meat in tight trousers;
they skipped leg day,
busying near the church.
It's refurbished red,
gold, gaudy god, confession fetish.
He will read you like a prophecy,
I am sure.
Our presence is fleeting and unsafe,
looking for rainbow flags.

Frankie

I like watching my cat drink water from the table.
She likes it in a pint, topped up and fresh.
We warn the guests *that's Frankie's glass.*
I watch her tentatively lean in, checking,
then greedily slurp; droplets from her chin glisten.
It reminds me of when she was a kitten;
she had an infection with blood in her urine.
It made me so anxious holding this creature
as she suffered; I was helpless, wanting to fix things.
Now I gaze at her closely, watch her run our routine,
this little thing roaming her kingdom.

Bluebells

You left your handprint
sinking into her arm.
It should have filled up
but you pinched her skin red.
Now we're stood in my flat years on
talking about why she's too scared
to walk through the bluebells alone.

Rabbit

She killed a rabbit today.
Tore it to shreds;
the glistening red spiralled like ribbon.
I screamed, the shrill echoing into an empty forest.
She looked at me as if to say
you lot get yours in a vacuum pack,
neat and arms-length,
like you didn't know it was murder.

Period Party

My pockets are snack pockets.
My face is rosy like gammon.
I bloat into the sky, floating like an abandoned balloon,
strap myself to the bed with three pillows and an
   ice-cream spoon.
I run to the toilet intermittently,
moaning, writhing and writing this poem.
It started days before,
skin crawling like spiders, libido higher than normal,
no tolerance for humans,
fending off friendships like wasps,
holding off tears at a party,
unmoved by everything,
you grumpy fuck.
I will spend the days motionlessly bleak,
sweating and farting myself to sleep.

V

HOLDING HANDS IN BED

Holding Hands in Bed

Sometimes there are no words,
just hands under white linen
under the dinner table
at an estranged family meal.
Our palms have a complementary feel,
a reassuring hold.
She tells me with worn lines, *you fit the mould;*
she tells me with warm cries,
you're a soft breeze in the blistering heat.
I want to make a family somehow
or find some kind of peace
so I pick my words carefully,
with grace, not rushing or pushing.
She holds my hand while we walk through the cemetery,
she holds my hand after we embrace.
We hold on to everything
when we are resting, and when we are awake.

Exmoor in Autumn

We drive slowly under sprawling trees,
my hand is wrapped between your knees,
the dappled light bursts into flames.
I want you more than ever.
Every part of the fire lives here.
Resting on rolling hills is auburn red,
glowing golds, saffron you can almost hold;
your straw-coloured strands
leave me heady and optimistic.
We take the long way home after a tumbling tour
and lie down together for our third November.

A&E

When you work nights
it's like we're on different sides of this world.
Your light is my dark,
my right side of the bed is hard and cold.
I can't watch the end of the show and pretend
I haven't seen it, because you'll know.
You will get first dibs on the pillows
when you get home.
And I know it's selfish, I respect what you do,
but I can't find anything on this earth
that makes it worth missing you.

Emily Dickinson

Susan, my dear,
our nights are wilder still;
when will our whispers end?
Letters link the wandering words,
ink disperses through Orion's belt.
Our connection forms life on the hem
of a distant landscape tilt.
Endless fields and endless yarns
are forged between us.
The neat cuffs hold tight the stranglehold of men.
The lineage of esteem stirs in a fortress womb.
Womankind is tied to a bed.
The linen you left is unwashed
so I look further within to clean;
my purity is a heart wrung upon a whitened sleeve.
It is sodden and heavy from our forever fate
that I can't love you openly
and be with you tonight.

Candlelit Clouds

I miss candlelit clouds
you collected for me.
And the rain that fell down on our landscape of sea.
I miss all the smells you caught in my breath,
the way your gentle skin on my head lay to rest.
And we'd rest for hours,
fit together like jigsaw made of human flesh; we had power.
When we kissed the sounds hissed like windswept beds of
    fresh flowers,
picked by the sky's fingertips to devour
a season-stained tower of colour on colour;
oh, how she missed that lady above her.

Open

I will let my thighs soften like bruised apples.
I will open.
I will let you be the one.
With guided hand the tension will unravel.
The vice will spin,
letting me become.

What I Can See

She's picking sea urchin out of my foot
with two lights,
a needle and a pair of tweezers searching expertly.
My ankle smells of vinegar.
Bending like stubborn oak,
we cut and dig at the weathered bits.
Let's make a prize out of poison.
There are four spikes
slung over her shoulder,
three to go,
stopping to drink and rest.

Their Place

My hand traces the line of your shoulder.
Your body is wound tight from long days and a brave face.
I get the Tiger Balm from the cabinet;
it's on an empty shelf.
Where does it hurt?
Your arm is around my waist, pulling me
from dusk; I am on my own at Christmas.
Our bodies are naked on the bed;
the summer is too hot,
so we hold hands instead.
There is space to open up,
the words form and find their place.

Winter

I'm playing Scrabble with my soulmate,
Alina, she's a fever and I'm flush all over.
We're searching the letters
to connect and find meaning.
It illuminates our features.
Under a tilting lampshade, I kiss her.
We bunker down together.
I'm keeping the heat up with the inside of my right thigh.
We lean, and fall in.
The winter is a test where our lights are dimmed,
my laugh is thin and empty.
But I like staying home when I can hear her,
the busying of a curry cauldron,
when she is getting ready, singing German punk songs.
I ask her what it all means;
she smiles and I feel complete.

Crescent

Three courts are open in spring,
tennis shorts and white nets rip the cool wind.
We sit next to chestnut trees that remind her of Munich.
We have moved into a crescent
where the moonlight is warm and the daytimes romantic.
There is a park full of people and dogs
and running routes; we plan our next jog with a promise of
    crumpets.
A new start. The wooden floors only creak for two hearts
and the road is quiet.
We promise love and peaceful pressing
lips in abundance, sharing bathtubs.
You ask me to visit behind the next door.
I watch your body and think about being with you forever.

Desire

There's a moment where bodies unravel,
taboo times ascend
in an ethereal fashion.
Your eyes address my thighs
exposed by desire, you come up for air.
Kissing in the shower, pushed against porcelain,
your breasts arrive at the beginning
of where I'm going.
I bite gently, searching, hearing your moaning.
I want you to say my name again into my hair.
Hands unfasten fast on the familiar parts of your woman.
Wetness falls from strands onto your neck.
You pull me closer to God.

Polari Press

Taking our name from the secret slang Polari, we are an independent publishing house which seeks out hidden voices and helps them be heard.

Although Polari was spoken almost exclusively by gay and bisexual men, the nature of clandestine meetings of the mid 1900s, when homosexuality was still criminalised, brought together people from all walks of life who all had an influence on the language.

Cockney, Romany and Italian languages mixed with the colloquialisms of thespians, circus performers, wrestlers, sailors and wider criminal communities to create a slang to express their sexuality secretly and safely.

Inspired by these origins, we publish queer voices as well as other marginalised groups, to share our perspectives with each other, and help build a collaborative platform for all of us.

polari.com